jWAY

Triceratops

by Daniel Cohen

Consultant:
Brent Breithaupt
Director
Geological Museum
University of Wyoming

Bridgestone Books
an imprint of Capstone Press
Mankato, Minnesota

Bridgestone Books are published by Capstone Press
151 Good Counsel Drive, P.O. Box 669, Mankato, Minnesota 56002
http://www.capstone-press.com

Library of Congress Cataloging-in-Publication Data
Cohen, Daniel, 1936–
      Triceratops/by Daniel Cohen.
      p. cm.—(The Bridgestone Science Library)
      Includes bibliographical references and index.
      Summary: Discusses the physical characteristics, habitat, food, defenses, relatives, and
      extinction of the Triceratops.
      ISBN 0-7368-0619-9
      1. Triceratops—Juvenile literature. [1. Triceratops. 2. The Bridgestone Science Library.]
      I. Title. II. Series.
QE862.O65 C628 2001
567.915′8—dc21   00-021738

Editorial Credits
Erika Mikkelson, editor; Linda Clavel, cover designer and illustrator; Heidi Schoof
  and Kimberly Danger; photo researchers

Photo Credits
Francois Gohier, cover, 10–11, 16
James P. Rowan, 8–9, 12
Richard Cummins, 14
Tom and Therisa Stack/TOM STACK & ASSOCIATES, 20
Visuals Unlimited/Ken Lucas, 4–5; A.J. Copley, 6

1 2 3 4 5 6 06 05 04 03 02 01

Table of Contents

Triceratops compared to a 5-foot-tall
(1.5-meter-tall) human

Triceratops

The name Triceratops
(try-SERR-ah-tops) means
three-horned face. Triceratops
looked like a rhinoceros.
But Triceratops was a large
dinosaur that weighed
6 tons (5.4 metric tons). It
measured 30 feet (9 meters)
from nose to tail.

The World of Triceratops

Triceratops lived between 72 million and 65 million years ago. The dinosaur lived in what is now North America. Many kinds of trees and flowering plants covered the land during the time Triceratops lived.

This dinosaur is Styracosaurus. Styracosaurus and Triceratops were ceratopsids.

Relatives of Triceratops

Triceratops belonged to a group of dinosaurs called ceratopsids (serr-a-TOP-sids). Ceratopsids had heavy bodies, big heads, and bony frills. Triceratops was the largest member of this group.

frill
a bony collar at the back of the neck of ceratopsids

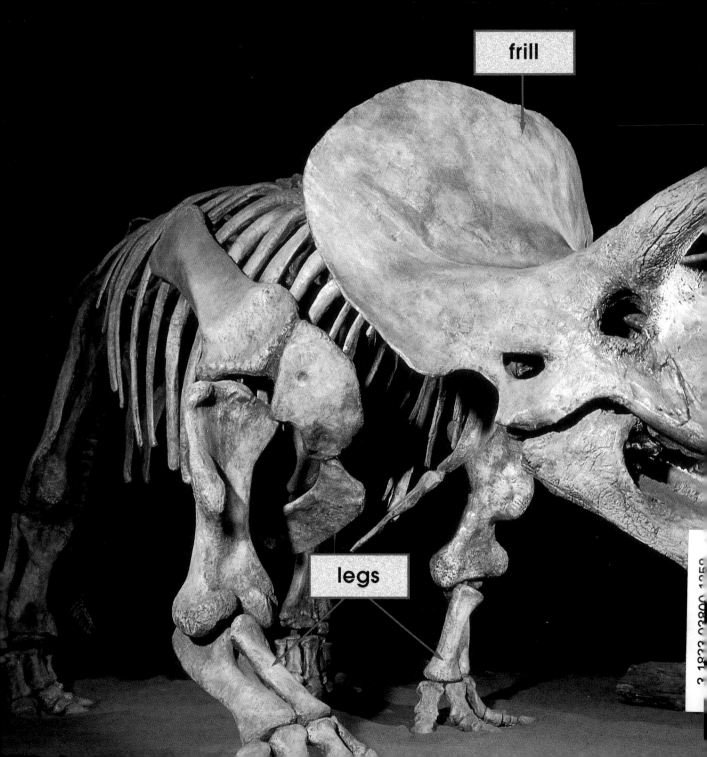

frill

legs

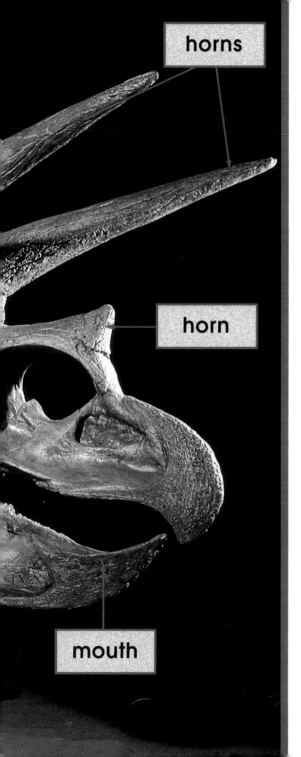

horns

horn

mouth

Parts of Triceratops

Triceratops had many parts that protected its body. Its huge head measured more than 6 feet (1.8 meters) long. It had a short, thick horn on its nose. Two larger horns stuck out above each eye. A neck frill fanned out at the back of its head. This bony collar protected Triceratops' neck.

What Triceratops Ate

Triceratops ate plants. It broke off leaves with its sharp, beak-like mouth and chewed them with its back teeth. Triceratops traveled in groups. They may have eaten all the plants in one area. The dinosaurs then moved to a new area to find more plants.

Predators

Predators such as Tyrannosaurus rex hunted Triceratops. Triceratops' horns, neck frill, and thick skin protected it. Some scientists think Triceratops ran very fast to escape predators. Triceratops may have reached speeds of 30 miles (48 kilometers) per hour.

predator
an animal that hunts and eats other animals

The End of Triceratops

Dinosaurs lived on Earth for more than 150 million years. All dinosaurs became extinct about 65 million years ago. Triceratops died out at this time. It probably was one of the last large dinosaurs to become extinct. Scientists are not sure why all the dinosaurs died.

extinct

no longer living anywhere in the world

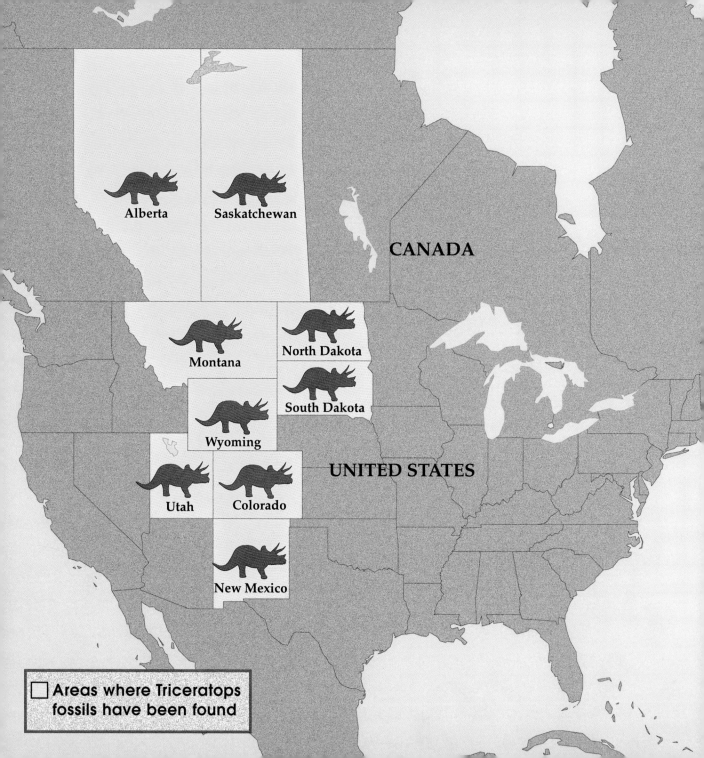

CANADA

Alberta

Saskatchewan

Montana

North Dakota

South Dakota

Wyoming

UNITED STATES

Utah

Colorado

New Mexico

☐ Areas where Triceratops
fossils have been found

Discovering Triceratops

In 1887, scientists first discovered Triceratops fossils near Denver, Colorado. In 1889, paleontologist Othniel Charles Marsh named the fossils Triceratops. Triceratops fossils have been found in many parts of the western United States and Canada.

paleontologist
a scientist who finds and studies fossils

Studying Triceratops Today

Paleontologists continue to study Triceratops fossils. They want to learn more about Triceratops and the world it lived in. Paleontologists want to know how Triceratops lived with one another.

Hands On: Dinosaur Footprints

When dinosaurs walked in mud or wet sand they left footprints. Some of these footprints became fossils after millions of years. Dinosaur footprint fossils give scientists information about how dinosaurs lived. You can learn how scientists study footprints.

What You Need

Dirt, snow, or wet sand
A group of friends
Several different kinds of shoes, sandals, or boots

What You Do

1. Find a stretch of wet sand, snow, or dirt.
2. Choose one person to be the scientist. The scientist hides. The other people are dinosaurs.
3. Some of the dinosaurs wear shoes, sandals, or boots. If the weather is warm enough, some dinosaurs can have bare feet. Walk, run, or crawl across the sand, snow, or dirt. The dinosaurs leave.
4. The scientist looks at the footprints. Which people ran? Which people walked? Who made each set of footprints?
5. Take turns being the scientist and the dinosaurs.

The footprints of people who run usually will be farther apart than the footprints of people who walked. The footprints of people who run also will be deeper than those of the people who walked.

Words to Know

dinosaur (DYE-na-sore)—an extinct land reptile; dinosaurs lived on Earth for more than 150 million years.

fossil (FOSS-uhl)—the remains or traces of something that once lived; bones and footprints can be fossils.

frill (FRILL)—the bony collar-like part at the back of ceratopsids' necks

paleontologist (PAY-lee-on-TOL-ah-jist)—a scientist who finds and studies fossils

scientist (SYE-uhn-tist)—a person who studies the world around us

Read More

Bergen, Lara Rice. *Triceratops.* Prehistoric Creatures Then and Now. Austin, Texas: Steadwell Books, 2000.

Landau, Elaine. *Triceratops.* A True Book. New York: Children's Press, 1999.

Riehecky, Janet. *Triceratops: The Horned Dinosaur.* New York: Benchmark Books, 1998.

Internet Sites

Kinetosaurs: Dinosaur Database
http://www.childrensmuseum.org/kinetosaur/e.html
Triceratops—Enchanted Learning Software
http://www.enchantedlearning.com/subjects/dinosaurs/dinos/Triceratops.shtml
Triceratops: Rhinoceros of Dinosaurs
http://www.letsfindout.com/subjects/dinosaurs/rtmtri.html

Index